Above: Fortuna, the Roman Goddess of fortune and fate, by Hans
Sebald Beham, 1541. She was worshipped extensively in Italy from the
earliest times and is the keeper of destiny, consulted for good fortunes
and prosperity. Often depicted bearing a cornucopia of abundance, a
spinner of destiny, and a ball representing the uncertainty of fortune.

US edition © 2024 by Jewels Rocka
Published by Wooden Books LLC,
San Rafael, California

First published in the UK in 2022
by Wooden Books Ltd, Glastonbury, UK

Library of Congress Cataloging-in-Publication Data
Rocka, J.
Divination

Library of Congress Cataloging-in-Publication
Data has been applied for

ISBN-10: 1-952178-12-6
ISBN-13: 978-1-952178-12-2

Designed and typeset in Glastonbury, UK

Printed in China on FSC® certified papers by
RR Donnelley Asia Printing Solutions Ltd.

DIVINATION

ELEMENTS OF WISDOM

Jewels Rocka

*Admiration and gratitude to all the seers who came before me, leaving
a wealth of technique and information by which to study and learn.
With special thanks to Clare Austin, who, quite apart from the
technical, editorial and moral support, has always helped me "see".
And as always thanks and appreciation to Richard Creightmore,
my partner in life, love and Geomancy.*

ABOVE: *An augur of Ancient Rome, employing Alectryomany (see p.20).
"The present moment is the only moment available to us,
and is the door to all moments" - Thich Nhat Hanh*

ABOVE: *Illustration by Edmond Lechevallier-Chevignard [1825-1902], showing the Greek goddess Ananke (Roman Necessitas, "necessity") as the supreme arbitrator of fate and circumstance. Holder of the cosmic spindle, she is the mother of the Moirai, the Three Fates representing destiny, fortune and inevitability; Clotho spins the thread, Lachesis measures the thread and Atropos cuts the thread.*

INTRODUCTION

THE HISTORY OF DIVINATION is long and vast. Since time immemorial humans have sought to understand their place in the universe, comprehend cycles of being, interpret their relationships, find meaning in their existence, gaze into the future and see the unseen. The term comes from the Latin *divinare*, "to foresee" or "receive messages from the gods".

The oldest and most comprehensive writings about divination come from the Chinese *Book of Changes*, the *Yi Jing* (c. 1142 BC), which details a style of prophesying that evolved from even older practices of casting bones into a fire and reading patterns on their charred surfaces.

Divination methods and ritual tools have developed with time, necessity and fashion, as people sought to find the best path, guarantee their crops or secure their futures. When seeking insights into political winds of change and other kinds of weather before an important marriage or battle, a soothsayer or shaman would be consulted to read the auguries in the intestines of sacrificed animals. Today we have other tools at hand, such as polls, predictive analytics and meteorology, but divination remains stubbornly popular, especially within personality and relationship dynamics.

Humans are by nature questing creatures, always seeking knowledge of potential tomorrows. Many people, especially in times of uncertainty or vulnerability, find that connecting with the greater plan can help them feel more accepting and in control of their lives. Divination shines a guiding light on a divinely recommended line of action to secure the best possible outcomes.

THE ELEMENTS OF DIVINATION
and the planes of being

THERE ARE MANY ancient divination tools and rituals for connecting to the divine. In this book they are grouped according to the four Aristotelian elements of western alchemy: *fire*, *earth*, *air* and *water*, plus the fifth element, *ether* (the binding force of nature). The five elements represent five different portals or pathways to divining the truth:

△ **FIRE**: *Casting*. The seeker performs a ritual in the moment to draw down wisdom, knowledge and information about their concern.

▽ **EARTH**: *Language of the Earth*. Observing physical cycles and natural patterns to gain clarity about something that is not yet manifest.

△ **AIR**: *Mapping and Measuring*. Using theoretical constructs and known patterns to calculate relationships and investigate the character of an entity or situation to gain insight and foretell likely futures.

▽ **WATER**: *Feeling the Vibes*. Connecting to the etheric energy of an object, situation or sensory clue to receive a picture or story.

◯ **ETHER**: *Heaven's Gift*. The seer is given information, sometimes unbidden, from the higher planes of awareness. Messages may come from astral beings, the mental or even spiritual planes.

Many metaphysical doctrines speak of interconnected planes of being or 'states of awareness' (*illustration opposite, the Sephirotic Tree of Life, Robert Fludd, 1621*). Understanding these subtleties gives insight and focus in divination work as you connect through these states to the subject or question under investigation. These planes are, loosely speaking:

THE SPIRITUAL PLANE: That which cannot be named. The 'great mystery' of unity from which all lower planes emanate and to which they return. Communion with this plane of pure conscious awareness, the *Turiya* in Sanskrit, can bestow flashes of events to come.

THE MENTAL PLANE: the fundamental patterns of the cosmos whereby all lower levels have their origins. The causal plane of natural law, abstract consciousness and logic, outside of space and time. It contains the symbols, colours and blueprints for all that we experience.

THE ASTRAL PLANE: the level of consciousness and the realm of dreams and imagination. Underlying forces, principles of nature and archetypes begin to take form here. Guides, gods and cosmic beings walk these planes, as do ideas and thought forms and constructions.

THE ETHERIC PLANE: the framework of subtle energies on which all material substance is arranged. Close to matter, it exists in time and space and can affect the material world. Easily accessible for divinatory enquiry and etheric aura readings.

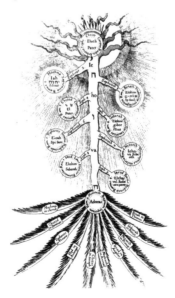

THE PHYSICAL PLANE: the state of material substance and level of manifestation, not the cause of embodiment. Everything physical is already patterned in the levels above, with the spiritual plane being the source of all being.

DIVINATORY PREPARATION
ritual for the divine

In divination, you are essentially searching for the truth. So prepare:

GROUND AND CLEAR yourself and your divinatory tools to add clarity and depth to a reading. Using dirty tools can corrupt a reading, so although you need not be squeaky clean—*"water which is too pure has no fish"*—attend to your psychic hygene. Quieten your mind, connect to the divine, and let go of pretentions and assumptions.

INVOKE SOME PROTECTION e.g. white light or guardian beings (*or see examples opposite*). Open channels attract all sorts of energy.

ASK THE RIGHT QUESTION for the chosen method of divination. Some techniques are better at eliciting a yes/no answer (e.g. dowsing), while others are better at delivering a narrative (e.g. tarot).

UNDERSTAND WHAT YOU ARE ACTUALLY ASKING. Correctly framing the question and exploring its nuances is one of the greatest skills of a seer, and is often easier to do when reading for another.

RELAX, AND LET THE "KNOWING" ARRIVE. The hallmark of a good seer is a true connection and the ability to spin a yarn or story in tune with the essence of the seeker and their question. The initial divinatory imagery which appears may suggest a quick answer, and with practice and connection the deeper message will sing to you with relevance.

4

Protection: Two safe ways of tuning into higher energy planes: LEFT: *The Magician draws down power and knowledge from the universe. On his table sit symbols of the elements, a Wand (fire), Pentacle (earth), Sword (air), and Cup (water). Imagine being inside one part of the infinity sign above his head while the item being probed is in the other part. Open the crossing of the infinity figure to channel the divine and then close it quickly when enough information is gained.*

RIGHT: *The High Priestess sits between the black and white pillars of the Temple of Solomon connecting heaven and earth. Solid and grounded, on her lap a scroll of esoteric wisdom, she holds her own space as she sits on her throne. When divining, imagine being between two connected pillars, then step out and open a channel with the divine, secure in the knowledge that if threatened in any way (e.g. see below) then you can return to the protection of the pillars.*

5

FIRE
divination by casting

FIRE CORRESPONDS TO SPIRIT, action, passion, desire and immediacy. In the ritual action of *casting* a seeker poses a question and by throwing, rolling or shaking, awakens the spirit surrounding the issue to reveal an answer. This is achieved through divine synchronicity, a coincidence between a well-cast question and a revealing outcome. Success requires a clearly formed question, posed with respect and reverence.

Divining through the element of fire is a popular technique. Originally the province of trained professional seers, it later became a popular method for dabblers and parlour games, running the risk of attracting lower astral energy, false readings and wilful misguidance.

With experience, however, a seer can learn the language of a chosen method and use the casting tools merely as a prompt to open the fire portal and access a far deeper reading.

Examples of casting systems are **DICE** *(p.14)*, **GEOMANCY** *(p.16)*, **RUNES** *(p.12)*, **TAROT** *(p.8)*, **TASSEOMANCY** *(see opposite)* and **YI JING** *(p.18)*.

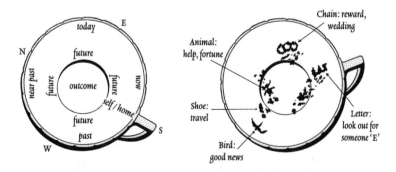

TASSEOMANCY is the ancient tradition of reading tea leaves, coffee grounds (Turkey) or wine lees (Rome). Bid the subject drink from a cup with a light interior while they think about their issues, until there is a little liquid left. Holding the cup in your non-dominant hand swirl it clockwise three times ensuring the liquid reaches the brim. Quickly turn the cup upside down on the saucer. Interpretation relies on creating a narrative from the association of the symbols.

Anchor: Success in business	Clumps: Busy life	Man, Woman: Love, Union
Animals: Unexpected assistance	Coffin, Bag: Illness, Trap	Oblongs: Family troubles
Arrow: Romance, Adventure	Cross: Kiss, Sorrow, Death	Question mark: Hesitancy; Caution
Bell: Unexpected news	Crown: Loyalty, Honor	Scissors: Closure, Broken bond
Birds: Freedom, Success, Good news	Cup: Reward; Fortune; Aid	Shoe: Journey, Change
Boat: Visit from a friend; Protection	Face: New people; Changes afoot	Snake: Wisdom, Enemy
Bridge: Healing, Opportunity	Finger: Look where it points	Squares: Peace, Happiness
Bush: New friends, Surprises	Fish: Good fortune from afar	Sun: Success, Power, Creativity
Chair: Unexpected Guest	Flowers, Leaf: Joy, Happiness	Sword, Dagger: Arguments, Enmity
Circle: Union, Money, Gifts	Gate, Doorway: Future success	Tower: Uncertainty, Change
Circle, broken: Delay	Hand: Open friend; closed foe	Tree: Strength, Health
Claw: Hidden Enemy	Heart: Happy, Friend, Love	Triangles: Journeys, Legacy
Clear around: Happiness	Horseshoe, Kite: Wishes come true	Waterfall: Flow, Prosperity
Clouds around: Sadness	Line, straight: Peace, Tranquility	Woodland: Beware of pitfalls
Clover: Luck, Wealth, Reward	Lines, long wavy: Loss, Frustration	Worms: Look to your health

Tarot
on the cards

No one really knows when the use of **TAROT** cards began. Some claim that as traders passed through ancient cities speaking different languages, they created a pictorial and evocative form of divination to convey shared meaning. Both the ancient Babylonians and the priests of Egypt practiced tarot, but the first recognisable cards appeared in the French courts around 1390, while the Occult tarot deck has stayed virtually the same since the 18th century.

Encoded and depicted on tarot cards is a world of symbols and imagery carrying a great wealth of ancient occult knowledge for the dedicated student. Even a reading using only key words as a prompt for a free flowing narrative can elicit powerful insight.

An Occult tarot deck consists of 78 cards made up of 22 Major Arcana cards and 56 Minor Arcana (suit cards) representing the four elements: **WANDS** (fire), **CUPS** (water), **SWORDS** (air), and **PENTACLES** (earth). It has also spawned many different versions, designed by artists, philosophers, astrologers and others, which include images of angels, aliens, animals, trees and so on.

All decks are read in a similar way, by casting shuffled cards or those chosen randomly into a variety of spreads, to analyse different aspects of life.

ABOVE: *Asking the cards. There are many types of spreads suited to different types of questions and lengths of time. The Celtic Cross layout is one classic divinatory spread (e.g. see page 12).*

ABOVE: *A three-card Tarot spread.*
This simple layout can represent past/present/future or any three designated qualities. In the case shown: in the past there has been a need for truth and balance; now there is some confusion or self-deception, caution is needed; the situation will be resolved, using courage and focus.

0 THE FOOL: Taking Risks; *Awareness*; start on a journey or adventure.

 1 THE MAGICIAN: Realising Powers; Crossroad of potential; paying attention.

 2 THE HIGH PRIESTESS: Wise Woman; Psychic ability; teaching; self-discovery.

 3 THE EMPRESS: Earthy Woman; Imagination; nurturing of creation; a child.

 4 THE EMPEROR: A Powerful Man; Authority; taking and giving counsel.

 5 THE HIEROPHANT: A High Priest; Traditional, reliable; ritual; re-evaluation.

 6 THE LOVERS: A Loving Relationship; Choice that may involve sacrifice.

 7 THE CHARIOT: Mastery of the Elements; Confrontation; obstacles to overcome.

 8 STRENGTH: Physical and Spiritual power; Heroism; courage and self-discipline.

 9 THE HERMIT: Inner Search for Wisdom; A secret revealed; withdrawal; silence.

 10 WHEEL OF FORTUNE: Unexpected events; Change is inevitable, can be good fortune.

 11 JUSTICE: A Balanced Virtue; Impartial Judgement; successful with law.

 12 THE HANGED MAN: A New Perspective; Transformation; sacrifice to make change .

 13 DEATH: Destruction and Renewal; Reincarnation; a major change.

 14 TEMPERANCE: Balance and Harmony; Moderation; self-control; patience.

 15 THE DEVIL: Delusion and Suffering; Bondage to others, concepts and objects.

 16 THE TOWER: Breakdown of Systems; Destruction; crisis; fall from grace.

 17 THE STAR: Bright Promises; Opportunity; hope; a wish come true.

 18 THE MOON: Not All is What it Seems; Delusion; deceit; hidden enemies; women.

 19 THE SUN: Successful and Fruitful; Expansive; creative; trusting; achievement.

 20 JUDGEMENT: Improvement in All Things; Second chances; being non judgemental.

 21 THE WORLD: Completion of All Things; Attainment; success; triumph; travel.

THE MAJOR ARCANA

ACE OF WANDS (FIRE): Exciting birth of an enterprise.

2 OF WANDS: A creative opportunity.

3 OF WANDS: Patience; strong foundations laid.

4 OF WANDS: Hard work leads to celebrations.

5 OF WANDS: Opposition; plans go wrong.

6 OF WANDS: Achievement; there is more to do.

7 OF WANDS: Competition; persevere, believe.

8 OF WANDS: Long term success; hectic times; travel.

9 OF WANDS: A challenge; strength of purpose.

10 OF WANDS: Lighten your load; take a step back.

KNIGHT OF WANDS: A curious young person; stimulating.

PAGE OF WANDS: Dynamic person; change; adventure.

QUEEN OF WANDS: Independent; enthusiastic; warm.

KING OF WANDS: Inspirational leader; creative.

ACE OF CUPS (WATER): New relationship; birth.

2 OF CUPS: Union; successful partnership; contact.

3 OF CUPS: Celebration; relief after difficulty.

4 OF CUPS: High expectations; resentment builds.

5 OF CUPS: Regret and sorrow; grief and acceptance.

6 OF CUPS: Something from the past; peaceful love.

7 OF CUPS: Many choices; calls to be realistic.

8 OF CUPS: A life chapter is over; walk away.

9 OF CUPS: Wishes come true; contentment; pleasure.

10 OF CUPS: Success after struggle; happy family.

KNIGHT OF CUPS: A romantic person; spiritual journey.

PAGE OF CUPS: A sensitive man; quest for love; proposal.

QUEEN OF CUPS: A sensitive woman; tuning into emotions.

KING OF CUPS: Experienced man; be open and affectionate.

ACE OF SWORDS (AIR): New concept; decision needed.

2 OF SWORDS: Face facts and confront fears; tension grows.

3 OF SWORDS: A painful realisation; arguments; betrayal.

4 OF SWORDS: Rest & recuperate after a difficult situation.

5 OF SWORDS: Know limitations; pushing creates conflict.

6 OF SWORDS: Conflict fades; easier times ahead.

7 OF SWORDS: Beware who you trust; diplomacy resolves.

8 OF SWORDS: Trapped by circumstances; patience.

9 OF SWORDS: Worry and anxiety; keeps fears in check.

10 OF SWORDS: Difficult end of cycle; revaluate; move on.

KNIGHT OF SWORDS: A sharp young person; read the small print

PAGE OF SWORDS: A brave assertive man; stand up for beliefs

QUEEN OF SWORDS: Perceptive woman; knowledge is power

KING OF SWORDS: Powerful man; expert opinion; stay calm.

ACE OF PENTACLES (EARTH): Material success; new business.

2 OF PENTACLES: Balance your time and finances.

3 OF PENTACLES: Early financial success; more to do

4 OF PENTACLES: Stuck and stagnant; reluctant to take risks

5 OF PENTACLES: See the big picture to overcome loss.

6 OF PENTACLES: An opportunity; faith rekindled; sharing.

7 OF PENTACLES: Revaluate in light of use of skills and ability.

8 OF PENTACLES: Opportunity to develop talents and new skills

9 OF PENTACLES: Contentment through material achievements.

10 OF PENTACLES: Financial and business success; happy family

2 OF PENTACLES: A talent to develop, a small windfall.

PAGE OF PENTACLES: Dependable; reliable; getting bogged down

QUEEN OF PENTACLES: Wise business woman; Attend material comforts.

KING OF PENTACLES: Top business man; count your blessings.

RUNES
and their meanings

The runic alphabet has been used widely in different forms for more than 2000 years in Northern Europe. Runes were used as symbols of knowledge for place names, writing, divination, healing and magic, forming sigils for luck, protection and love. The word comes from the Old Norse *runa*, 'secret' or 'whisper', and Old Irish Gaelic *run*, 'mystery'. The characters were formed of straight lines, making them suitable for burning or carving into bone, stone, tiles or wood (*see opposite*).

The runes can be drawn or cast in a variety of spreads (*e.g. see below*), connecting the seeker to a great lineage of divination. Consulting the runes will give answers requiring vision and interpretation.

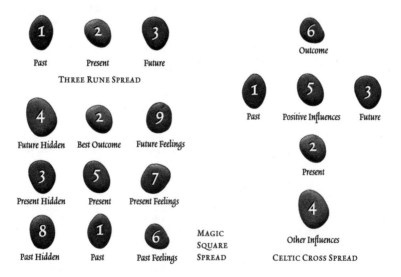

ᚢ U URUZ
WILD OX: *strength, raw energy, changes, rebirth*

ᚠ F FEHU
CATTLE: *wealth, fulfilment, success, abundance, fertile*

ᚦ TH THURISAZ
GIANT: *gateway, force, conflict, wait, abundance*

ᚨ A ANSUZ
GOD STONE: *divine breath, signs, luck, advice*

ᚱ F RAIDO
WAGON: *travel, journeys, work, having perspective*

ᚲ K KANO
BEACON: *light, revelation, inspiration, creative, vitality*

ᚷ G GEBO
GIFT: *generosity, balance, exchanges, relationships*

ᚹ W WUNJO
JOY: *comfort, pleasure, clarity, ecstasy, restoration*

ᚺ H HAGALAZ
HAIL: *natural forces, crisis, destruction, trial, awakening*

ᚾ N NAUTHIZ
NEED; *delay, resistance, restriction, self-reliance*

ᛁ I ISA
ICE: *challenge, frustration standstill, stop and reflect*

ᛃ J,Y JERA
YEAR: *good harvest, peace fruition, full cycle, timeliness*

ᛇ EI EIHWAZ
YEW TREE: *defence, honest endurance, stable, reliable*

ᛈ P PERTH
HIDDEN: *secrets, initiation, occult, women's business*

ᛉ Z,R ALGIZ
ELK: *protections, a shield, defence, guardians, beware*

ᛋ S SOWELU
SUN: *life force, victory, power, completion, health*

ᛏ T TEIWAZ
TYR -Sky God: *leadership, authority, honour, justice*

ᛒ B BERKANA
BIRCH GODDESS: *fertility, birth, growth, renewal*

ᛖ E EHWAZ
HORSES: *moving forward, change, progress, transport*

ᛗ M MANWAZ
HUMANITY: *self or others, social order, interaction*

ᛚ L LAGUZ
WATER: *ebb & flow, renewal, sea, dreams, astral journeys*

ᛜ G INGUZ
ING-EARTH GOD: *gestation, completion, rest and relief*

ᛞ D DAGUZ
DAY: *dawn, awakening, growth, clarity, hope*

ᛟ O OTHILA
ANCESTRAL INHERITANCE: *karma, property, values, culture*

ABOVE: *The 24 runes of the Elder Futhark alphabet. A full set often includes a 25th blank rune:*
WYRD — UNKNOWABLE: *fate, the end is empty, as is the beginning.*

Dice

shake, rattle and roll

Astragalomancy, divination with dice, takes its name from 'astragali', knuckle bones. The practice dates back to at least 4000 BC, long before it became an obsession with the citizens of Ancient Rome. Wealthy Roman wives would gather at the Temple of the Vesta to consult the dice for their fortunes. Believing the Gods to show favour through luck, gambling on dice games became such a popular pastime that it was banned, except at festivals such as Saturnalia.

Dice divination is still used by the Roma people, and is useful for its succinct answers to tight questions, including further casts for elaboration and clarification to probe the heart of a question.

Casting with three six-sided dice is standard (although dice of 4, 8, 10, 12, 20 or 30 sides can be used).

The die may be cast on a round mat, or 12-inch chalked circle. Dice falling outside the circle can either be ignored, or render the cast null and void, or signify extra meaning.

The face value of the cast dice are added, and the sum is then reduced to a single digit (e.g. for a throw of 3:5:6, 3 + 5 + 6 = 11, and 1 + 1 = 2, so look up the reading for 2.

Relax, focus on your question and let the dice fall where they may.

ASTRAGALOMANCY	TWO DICE	THREE DICE

ASTRAGALOMANCY	TWO DICE	THREE DICE
	1 – Yes	3 – Change for the better
	2 – No	4 – Disappointment
	3 – Beware	5 – Joy; Surprise; Success
	4 – Reflect	6 – Bad luck; Material Loss
	5 – Good luck	7 – Behind you; Scandal
	6 – Certainly	8 – Tread carefully
ONE DICE	7 – Have faith	9 – Love; Gambling; Unions
	8 – Be patient	10 – Births; Opportunities
Odd – Yes	9 – Absolutely	11 – Parting; Illness; Travel
Even – No	10 – Doubtful	12 – A message; Seek counsel
	11 – Nonsense	13 – Sorrow; Change
1 – Evaluate; Good luck	12 – Slight chance	14 – New Friend; Help arrives
2 – Success depends on others		15 – Stay still; Beware
3 – Victory		16 – Rewarding journey
4 – Disappointment		17 – Flexibility; Advice
5 – Great news		18 – Happiness, Success
6 – Uncertainty		

LEFT: **SANGOMA BONES** *represent human characters and the positive and negative forces influencing their lives.*

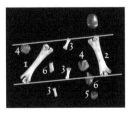

ABOVE RIGHT: *Romance and fertility is shown by the negative and positive forces lying between the man (1) and the woman (2). Positive forces - ancestor spirits (4) and eyes (6) - lie between the couple. There are also children bones (3) lying near the woman bone. A good indication of a romantic and fruitful relationship. Positive forces trump negative forces - crocodiles (5).*

GEOMANCY
the earth oracle

Oracular **GEOMANCY** has been in use for millennia across Africa, Arabia, Europe and Asia. Random marks are created by throwing handfuls of earth onto the ground, or by striking sand with a stick. Patterns of odd or even numbers then generate one or two dots respectively. Performing this four times creates one of sixteen binary tetragrams (*shown opposite*) to give a reading. A full geomantic shield may be drawn up by creating four of these tetragrams which represent the four 'mothers' (*below*).

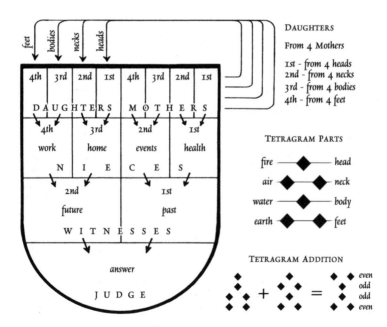

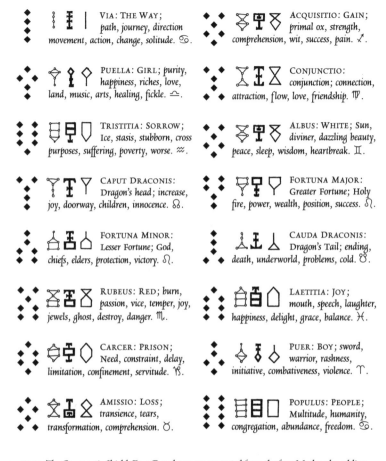

VIA: THE WAY; *path, journey, direction* movement, action, change, solitude. ♋.

PUELLA: GIRL; *purity, happiness, riches, love,* land, music, arts, healing, fickle. ♎.

TRISTITIA: SORROW; Ice, stasis, stubborn, cross purposes, suffering, poverty, worse. ♒.

CAPUT DRACONIS: Dragon's head; increase, joy, doorway, children, innocence. ☊.

FORTUNA MINOR: Lesser Fortune; God, chiefs, elders, protection, victory. ♌.

RUBEUS: RED; *burn,* passion, vice, temper, joy, jewels, ghost, destroy, danger. ♏.

CARCER: PRISON; Need, constraint, delay, limitation, confinement, servitude. ♑.

AMISSIO: LOSS; transience, tears, transformation, comprehension. ♉.

ACQUISITIO: GAIN; *primal ox, strength,* comprehension, wit, success, pain. ♐.

CONJUNCTIO: conjunction; connection, attraction, flow, love, friendship. ♍.

ALBUS: WHITE; Sun, diviner, dazzling beauty, peace, sleep, wisdom, heartbreak. ♊.

FORTUNA MAJOR: Greater Fortune; Holy fire, power, wealth, position, success. ♌.

CAUDA DRACONIS: Dragon's Tail; ending, death, underworld, problems, cold. ☋.

LAETITIA: JOY; mouth, speech, laughter, happiness, delight, grace, balance. ♓.

PUER: BOY; sword, warrior, rashness, initiative, combativeness, violence. ♈.

POPULUS: PEOPLE; Multitude, humanity, congregation, abundance, freedom. ♋.

LEFT: *The Geomantic Shield. Four Daughters are generated from the four Mothers by adding lines, with odd sums as* ◆ *and even sums as* ◆ ◆. *In the same way, the nieces etc are generated. The First Witness is Father of the Judge and reveals past testimony. The Second Witness is Mother of the Judge and reveals future testimony. The Judge answers the original question. A 'reconciler' may also be formed by adding the judge to the first mother, to clarify the judgement.*

YI JING
the oracle of changes

The central wisdom of the ancient Chinese **YI JING** (or I Ching) is that all beings and things have the capacity to adapt or change. Traditionally cast with yarrow stalks during an elaborate ritual (*see illustration below*), today the Yi Jing is more commonly cast using three identical coins, thrown six times to build a hexagram consisting of six lines:

− −	*Yin; 2 tails, 1 head.*	−×−	*Old Yin; 3 heads.*
——	*Yang; 2 heads, 1 tail.*	—○—	*Old Yang; 3 tails.*

The hexagram is compiled from the bottom up, and a commentary studied. Finally, any Old Yin and Old Yang 'changing' lines convert to their opposite to produce a second hexagram which is also studied.

line 6
line 5
line 4
line 3
line 2
line 1

upper trigram
lower trigram

upper trigram
lower trigram

1	34	5	26	11	9	14	43
25	51	3	27	24	42	21	17
6	40	29	4	7	59	64	47
33	62	39	52	15	53	56	31
12	16	8	23	2	20	35	45
44	32	48	18	46	57	50	28
13	55	63	22	36	37	30	49
10	54	60	41	19	61	38	58

ABOVE: *Construction of a hexagram, showing how Old Yin and Old Yang 'changing lines' flip into their opposites.*
RIGHT: *Table for finding hexagrams in the list below.*

1. *Qian.* The Creative. Perseverance brings success.

2. *Kun.* The Receptive. Follow subtle guidance for fortune.

3. *Tun.* Sprouting. Fragility at the beginning, persevere.

4. *Meng.* Youthful Folly. Success, tempered enthusiasm.

5. *Xu.* Waiting. Good outcome with politeness and prudence.

6. *Song.* Dispute. Conflict. Compromise and take advice.

7. *Shi.* The Multitude. Troops follow responsible leader.

8. *Bi.* Alliance. Cooperation encourages others to join.

9. *Xiao Chu.* Small harvest. Restrain and attend to details.

10. *Lu.* Walking. Continuing good conduct brings success.

11. *Tai.* Greatness. Peaceful prosperity, unite in harmony.

12. *Pi.* Obstruction. Standstill resulting from selfishness.

13. *Tong Ren.* Fellowship. Group effort brings profit.

14. *Da You.* Great Possessions. Huge wealth, offer charity.

15. *Qian.* Modesty. Reverence and offerings can harmonize.

16. *Yu.* Enthusiasm. Excess, pleasure, planned movement.

17. *Sui.* Following. Experience. To rule, first learn to serve.

18. *Gu.* Correction. Decay. Work on what has been spoiled.

19. *Lin.* Approach. Forest. Advancing brings great success.

20. *Guan.* Observation. Contemplation. Looking up.

21. *Shi He.* Biting through. Chew through problems.

22. *Bi.* Adornment. Minor success with refinement.

23. *Bo.* Stripping. Vulnerability. Splitting apart. Stay at home.

24. *Fu.* Return. Turning point. Movement is advantageous.

25. *Wu Wang.* Innocence. Unexpected pestilence.

26. *Da Chu.* Great Restraint. Tame your energy. Charity.

27. *Yi.* Nourishment. Attend to comfort and security.

28. *Da Guo.* Great Excess. Measures beyond the ordinary.

29. *Kan.* Abyss. Gorge. Repeated entrapment.

30. *Li.* Radiance. The clinging net. Balanced action profits.

31. *Xian.* Influence. Wooing. Conjoining brings joyful success.

32. *Heng.* Constancy. Endure and persevere for success.

33. *Dun.* Retiring. Yielding hides assets. Modesty.

34. *Da Zhuang.* Great Maturity. Intelligent invigorating power.

35. *Jin.* Advance. Flourishing prosperous progress, caution.

36. *Ming Yi.* Obscured light. Hidden intelligence. Modesty.

37. *Jia Ren.* Family. Virtue and responsibilities all in order.

38. *Kui.* Strange. Unusual Perversion. Opposition.

39. *Jian.* Difficulty. Limping. Obstruction. Seek wise counsel.

40. *Jie.* Loosen. Untangle for deliverence. Let goals arrive.

41. *Sun.* Decrease. Sacrifice. Sincerity and inner offering.

42. *Yi.* Increase. Actions bring earthly and spiritual flowering.

43. *Quai.* Decision. Decisive breakthrough and action.

44. *Gou.* Coupling. Meeting with a powerful female.

45. *Cui.* Clustering. Gathering. Strength in numbers. Support.

46. *Sheng.* Ascending. Tender lifting. The able shall rise.

47. *Kun.* Entanglement: Siege, confinement, fatigue, distress.

48. *Jing.* The Well. Selfless service and mutual care.

49. *Ge.* Reform. Revolution. Transformation with confidence.

50. *Ding.* Cauldron. Innovation, and recruitment. Creativity.

51. *Zhen.* Arousing. Thunder. Move calmly to face a challenge.

52. *Gen.* Stilling. Movement and pausing. Self restraint.

53. *Jian.* Infiltrating. Gradual advancement by degrees.

54. *Gui Mei.* Marrying maiden. Submission to destiny.

55. *Feng.* Abundance. Excess. Maintenance of acheivements.

56. *Lu.* Travelling. Developing outwardly in adversity.

57. *Xun.* Wind. Gently enter. Unobtrusive undertakings.

58. *Dui.* Joy. Persuasion. Speaking and encouragement.

59. *Huan.* Disperse. Expand and dissolve for gain. Reunify.

60. *Jie.* Moderation. Articulate and restrict when appropriate.

61. *Zhong Fu.* Inner Sincerity. Trust radiates from the heart.

62. *Xiao Guo.* Small exceeding. Great fortune from small details.

63. *Ji Ji.* Already Completed. Amicable and gracious dealings.

64. *Wei Ji.* Not Yet Completed. No profit until the end.

EARTH

show me a sign

THE **EARTH** ELEMENT relates to the tangible world of matter, practical concerns and the senses. It gives substance to the natural rhythms by which we live, e.g. the cycles of days, moon phases and seasons. Over time these and other events, including anomalies of life and the quirks of chance, have become associated with various outcomes that can be interpreted as supportive or detrimental to a situation.

Some historic methods are too brutal or unsavoury to use today (e.g. animal sacrifice and reading entrails), while other earth associations, rooted in the customs and beliefs of a particular place and time, will have passed from common use to superstition, and then been forgotten.

Earth readings feature strongly in love divination, assessing the quality of a relationship and foretelling the nature of major social and political changes. They are often used for simple yes/no answers, e.g. pulling the petals from a daisy, saying "he loves me, he loves me not".

Earth divination includes **AEROMANCY** (*p.26*), **HYDROMANCY** (*p.27*), **OMENS** (*opposite*) and divination with **FOOD** (*p.24*) or **ANIMALS** (*p.22*).

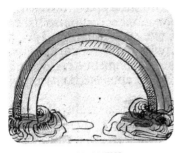

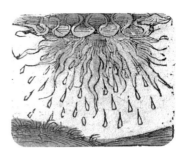

GOOD OMENS

Four-leafed clover - Meeting a sheep - Seeing a ladybird - Horseshoes in the U position - Wishbones - Bats at twilight - Walking in the rain - Gift of a beehive - Pod with nine peas - A robin flies into the house - Hearing crickets - Seeing a white butterfly - Burning your fingernail clippings - Cutting your hair during a storm - Finding a pin and hanging it on a hook - Seeing a load of hay - Seeing the New Moon over your right shoulder - Picking up a nail that was pointing towards you - Finding a pencil in the street - Keeping a piece of oyster shell in your pocket - Carrying a rabbit's foot - Sleeping on un-ironed sheets - Spilling your drink while proposing a toast - A sprig of white heather - Seeing a blue bird - A strange dog follows you home - Putting a dress on inside out - Rubbing two horseshoes together - Catching two rats in the same trap - Sneezing three times before breakfast - Meeting a chimney sweep - Well-swept doorways - Bird droppings land on you - Someone spills water behind you - Hearing the word 'rabbit' - The number 8 - Newly planted trees

BAD OMENS

An owl hoots three-times - A five-leafed clover - Peacock feathers indoors - Opening an umbrella indoors - Rooster crowing at night - Emptying ashes after dark - Bringing in eggs after dark - A hat on a bed - Giving away a wedding present - Giving scissor, knives or a clock as a present - Borrowing, lending or burning a broom - Cutting your nails on Friday - Bringing white lilac or hawthorn blossom into the house - New shoes on a chair or table - Killing a seagull, a spider or a cricket - Mending a garment while wearing it - Dropping an umbrella - An owl in daytime - Sleeping with a shelf over you - Meeting a grave digger - A button in the wrong hole - A picture falling - Breaking a glass during a toast - Dropping a glove - A ring breaking on your finger - Removing your wedding ring - Three butterflies together - Red and white flowers in the same arrangement - Putting your shirt on inside out - Walking under a ladder - Breaking a mirror - Walking over three drains - Walking over a crack - Letting a black cat cross your path - Stepping on a grate - Pointing at a rainbow

ABOVE: An omen prophesises something yet to happen. With a question in mind simply keep your eyes open and let the cosmos supply the answer. The skill in interpreting an omen is in making the signs and symbols relevant, using symbology, signs and correspondences. LEFT: In many cultures, the appearance of a comet or eclipse heralds a dire warning from the gods.

ANIMAL BEHAVIOUR
and interesting itches

Seers consider animals as pure embodiments of original spirit. Animals may therefore be closely observed to obtain valuable oracular clues.

AILUROMANCY is the study of cats. In most cultures a black cat crossing your path, particularly right to left, is seen as an unfortunate sign, although it is lucky in Britain. Similarly, a cat washing its face, climbing the furniture or sleeping with its back to the fire denotes rain.

ALECTRYOMANCY is the art of fortune-telling with a chicken. A seer would scatter some corn on an alphabet drawn in a circle, and then watch the rooster peck at the grains to spell out a message.

ARACHNOMANCY is divination using spiders. Various West African tribes observe the way spiders move small cards made from dried flat leaves which are marked with symbols and left outside their holes.

Another form of Earth divination is **TELAESTHESIA**. According to the Australian Aborigines of the Western Desert region, when you get an itch, pain or other body sensation it can give you information, *Punka-Punkara*, about a distant object, people or events. Equivalent systems were popular across Europe for thousands of years up to the modern period. Next time you get an itch, consult the diagram (*opposite*).

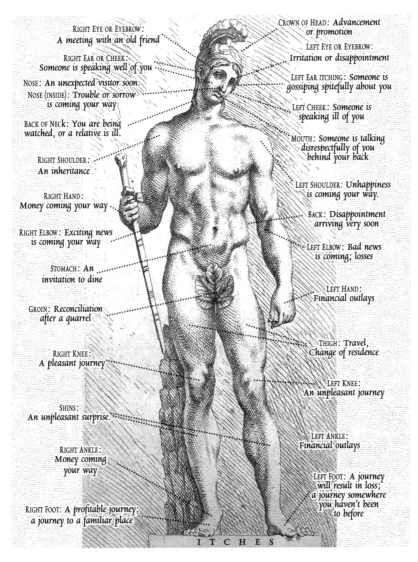

RIGHT EYE OR EYEBROW:
A meeting with an old friend

RIGHT EAR OR CHEEK:
Someone is speaking well of you

NOSE: An unexpected visitor soon.
NOSE (INSIDE): Trouble or sorrow
is coming your way

BACK OF NECK: You are being
watched, or a relative is ill.

RIGHT SHOULDER:
An inheritance

RIGHT HAND:
Money coming your way

RIGHT ELBOW: Exciting news
is coming your way

STOMACH: An
invitation to dine

GROIN: Reconciliation
after a quarrel

RIGHT KNEE:
A pleasant journey

SHINS:
An unpleasant surprise.

RIGHT ANKLE:
Money coming
your way

RIGHT FOOT: A profitable journey;
a journey to a familiar place

CROWN OF HEAD: Advancement
or promotion

LEFT EYE OR EYEBROW:
Irritation or disappointment

LEFT EAR ITCHING: Someone is
gossiping spitefully about you

LEFT CHEEK: Someone is
speaking ill of you

MOUTH: Someone is talking
disrespectfully of you
behind your back

LEFT SHOULDER: Unhappiness
is coming your way.

BACK: Disappointment
arriving very soon

LEFT ELBOW: Bad news
is coming; losses

LEFT HAND:
Financial outlays

THIGH: Travel,
Change of residence

LEFT KNEE:
An unpleasant journey

LEFT ANKLE:
Financial outlays

LEFT FOOT: A journey
will result in loss;
a journey somewhere
you haven't been
to before

ITCHES

23

Fortunes from Food
sorting good apples from bad

Holidays and feasts are popular occasions for seasonal divination.

FAVOMANCY, a spring festival divination from peas and beans, involves placing a bean in a dish of peas to be served with the main meal. The one who finds the bean in their portion gets the good luck.

KARUOMANCY, divination from nuts, is practised in Nigeria, where sixteen nuts are shaken between the hands and the pattern of odd and even numbers studied. Other traditions observe the behaviour of nuts jiggling or exploding in the embers of a fire or on a hotplate.

CROMNIMANCY was once very widespread and involves attaching names to different onions and then watching the way they each sprout.

ALEUROMANCY, performed in ancient Egypt, involves pouring flour out in small heaps and interpreting the shapes produced.

APPLES play a big role in love divination, e.g. at the Nov 1st Festival of Pomona, the Roman Goddess of orchards, when a spiral of apple peel thrown over the shoulder can reveal a letter on the ground, and apple seeds named and tossed in the fire or stuck to a face may reveal even more.

FORTUNE TELLING CAKE SET

Parties, Birthdays, Weddings, Valentine, New Years, Halloween

DIRECTION:
1. Distribute each charm in cake batter or place in cake after it is baked or bought.
2. The charms can also be drawn out of a glass or other receptacle if you do not wish to use the cake.
3. Then look at card for meaning.

TEA POT
This little teapot really does say Good Luck for some one far away.

FISH
This little fish is full of cheer. You'll soon see someone you'll love dear.

MOTORCYCLE
You'd better get used to lots of noise, for you'll have a large family of girls and boys.

RING
It isn't very hard to see that lucky in love you'll always be.

BOAT
This boat will start things humming. A happy engagement is soon forthcoming.

BANJO
Don't bother with love for pity's sake. An excellent musician you're sure to make.

BIRD CAGE
Listen to this bird whenever sad. It will make you happy and glad.

CHAIR
Don't envy others who are good-looking. You'll be more popular with your cooking.

PLANE
This plane never will tarry for soon you are to marry.

HORSE RACE
Racing today is all the swing. Tomorrow you'll wear a wedding ring.

FOR PARTIES AND FESTIVE OCCASIONS OF ALL KINDS, AMUSING AND ENTERTAINING.

ABOVE: A 1950s fortune cake set with rhyming captions. Left. 1878 Japanese senbei cooking. Chinese fortune cookies became popular in San Francisco c.1900. They contain slips of paper inscribed with different fortunes baked into dough balls.

FACING PAGE: Apple ducking and bobbing, traditional Halloween games dating back to Roman times and the Festival of Pomona.

AEROMANCY
in the wind and the water

AEROMANCY interprets events in the sky as divine messages—winds, storms, clouds, rainbows, comets and shooting stars. Europeans once associated thunder in the east with bloodshed, while high winds at Christmas foretold the death of a king. The Etruscans and Babylonians both saw thunder and lightning as signs of foreboding. Hindus interpreted the shapes made in clouds, still a popular pastime today.

Cloud images are often very personal to the reader, with no two interpretations of shapes being the same. They give insight into the state of one's mind and can help the seer tap into the streams of future consciousness to illuminate possibilities.

Angels offer you guidance; *Babies* suggest new beginnings; *Cats* ask you to expand your psychic abilities; *Circles* mean completion; *Buildings* reveal your self-worth; *Dancers* invite you to move; *Dragons* foretell success; *Hearts* speak of love is in the air; *Horses* signal reliability and freedom; *Rabbits* are symbols of fun; *Snakes* warn of deceit or danger.

The effects of wind on everyday objects can also message a seeker, whether ringing bells, flapping flags or paper on the wind. To divine a yes or no answer, use two identical pieces of paper marked yes and no. Ask your question as you release the papers into the wind from a height. The first to flutter to the ground will give you your answer.

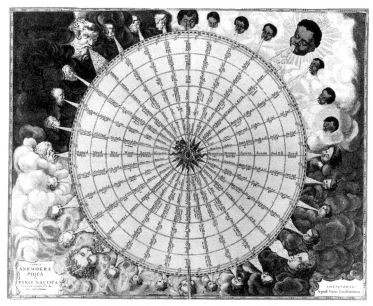

ABOVE: *The Compass of the Winds, Jan Jansson, 1650, showing 32 different personifications of the wind, depending on where it blows from. A simple wind divination tool may be constructed with such a dial to take instant readings from the wind. The Greek poet Homer refers to four winds, Boreas (north), Eurus (east), Notos (south) and Zephyrus (west).*

ABOVE: *The Chinese Emperor was given his morning reading via a singing bowl. The water was vibrated by rubbing the handles and the ripples were then studied.*

LEFT: **HYDROMANCY** *involves observing the shapes, colours, patterns, and sounds of water in the sea, springs or ponds. The Pitjantjatjara people of Central Australia select a pebble and rub it under their armpit before throwing it into a waterhole. If this produces clear strong ripples it is okay to stay, but if the stone produces little or no ripples then you'd better be away.*

AIR
mapping and measuring

THE ELEMENT OF **AIR** is associated with thought, logic, communication, theories and systematic knowledge. Divination through this portal is analytical. Theoretical constructs are used to calculate and interpret cycles and relationships, to analyse the character or nature of an entity or situation and to predict likely futures based on predictable cycles, patterns and correspondences. These techniques lend themselves to deep analysis of situations, character and personality and the election of favourable timings or locations.

From the 18th century, emerging scientific concepts in astronomy, medicine, physics, chemistry and philosophy undermined these ancient systems. Nevertheless, an interest in many of them persists to this day and has evolved, e.g. modern computers have made the arduous task of mapping and calculating cycles much easier. The many books, websites and workshops on these subjects is evidence of the continuing interest in such structured analysis of our existence.

Divinatory tools and tables are used to map and measure cycles and correspondences in disciplines such ASTROLOGY (*p.32*), PALMISTRY (*p.31*), PHYSIOGNOMY (*p.30*), NINE STAR KI (*p.36*), SELENOMANCY (*p.34*) and NUMEROLOGY (*opposite*).

SIMPLE ENGLISH			VALUE	GREEK			HEBREW		ARABIC		COMPLEX ENGLISH
a	j	s	1	A	α	alpha	א	aleph	١	'alif	A
b	k	t	2	B	β	beta	ב	bet	ب	ba	B
c	l	u	3	Γ	γ	gamma	ג	gimmel	ج	jim	C
d	m	v	4	Δ	δ	delta	ד	dalet	د	dal	D
e	n	w	5	E	ε	epsilon	ה	he	ه	ha	E
f	o	x	6	F	ϛ	digamma	ו	vov	و	waw	F
g	p	y	7	Z	ζ	zeta	ז	zayin	ز	za	G
h	q	z	8	H	η	eta	ח	het	ح	ha	H
i	r		9	Θ	θ	theta	ט	tet	ط	ta	I
			10	I	ι	iota	י	yod	ي	ya	J
			20	K	κ	kappa	כ	kof	ك	kaf	K
			30	Λ	λ	lambda	ל	lamed	ل	lam	L
			40	M	μ	mu	מ	mem	م	mim	M
			50	N	ν	nu	נ	nun	ن	nun	N
			60	Ξ	ξ	ksi	ס	samekh	ص س	sin/sad	O
			70	O	ο	omicron	ע	ayin	ع	'ayn	P
			80	Π	π	pi	פ	pé	ف	fa	Q
			90	Ϙ	ϙ	qoppa	צ	tsade	ض ص	sad/dad	R
			100	P	ρ	rho	ק	quf	ق	qaf	S
			200	Σ	σ	sigma	ר	resh	ر	ra	T
			300	T	τ	tau	ש	shin	س ش	shin/sin	U
			400	Υ	υ	upsilon	ת	tav	ت	ta	V
			500	Φ	φ	phi	ך	kof	ث	tha	W
			600	X	χ	chi	ם	mem	خ	kha	X
			700	Ψ	ψ	psi	ן	nun	ذ	dhal	Y
			800	Ω	ω	omega	ף	pé	ظ ض	dad/dha	Z
			900	ϡ	ϡ	san	ץ	tsade	غ ظ	dha/ghayn	
			1000						غ ش	ghayn/shin	

LEFT: *GEMATRIA Table. In the ancient world, letters stood for numbers, so every word was also a number. Many ancient texts (e.g. the Kabbalah, the Bible and the Quran) encode secret meanings using the interplay between letters and numbers (e.g. Jesus, ΙΗΣΟΥΣ, is 888).*

For your "Life Path Number" add the numbers in your birth date until they reduce to one of the 11 numbers below (e.g. 22.10.1991 →
2+2+1+1+9+9+1= 25
→ 2+5 =7.

For your "Character Number" add the numbers of the letters in your name using the Simple English table top left. Also analyse addresses, pet names and other key words in your life.

NUMEROLOGY - THE MEANING OF NUMBERS

ELEVEN NUMBERS ARE USED: 1–9, 11 & 22.

1 - BEGINNINGS: *leader, pioneer, innovator*

2 - PARTNERSHIP: *perfectionist, teamwork, mediator*

3 - GROWTH: *optimistic, versatile, good humoured*

4 - STABILITY: *determined, practical, conservative*

5 — SOCIAL: *creative, traveller, charming*

6 — LOVE: *affectionate, successful, indulgent*

7 — SPIRITUAL: *intuitive, sensitive, aloof*

8 — SECURITY: *hard-working, ambitious, organiser*

9 — DYNAMIC: *visionary, impatient, independence*

11 — STRENGTH: *idealistic, inspired, communicator*

22 — PERFECTION: *capable, talented, wise*

PHYSIOGNOMY
palmistry and moleoscopy

PHYSIOGNOMY is the art of assessing someone's character or disposition from their appearance, especially their face It is a fundamental facet of Chinese medicine and fortune-telling. The ancient Greek physician Hippocrates [460-370 BC] described how the excess or deficiency of any the four humours, which were believed to regulate the human body, could be read in someone's face (*see below*).

MOLEOSCOPY was also described by Hippocrates, although it predates both the Ancient Greek and Chinese cultures. The placement and quality of moles on the body enable a reading of character and fortune (*see table opposite*). It became hugely popular during the 16th and 17th centuries when elaborate maps and interpretations were developed, linking the position of moles on the body with astrology.

PHELGMATIC   CHOLERIC   SANGUINE   MELANCHOLIC

A GENUINE HUSBAND   AN UNRELIABLE HUSBAND   A GENUINE MOTHER   AN UNRELIABLE MOTHER

APPEARANCE OF MOLES

ROUND *Good character* ✳ ANGULAR *Bad character* ✳ OVAL *Bad luck* ✳ OBLONG *Prosperity* ✳ RAISED *Good fortune* ✳ GETTING LIGHTER *Luck improving* ✳ BECOMING DARKER *Trouble* ✳ HONEY/RED *Good luck* ✳ BLACK *Bad luck* ✳ TWO NEARBY *Two marriages; affairs* ✳ TWO, SYMMETRICAL *Dual nature*

MOLES ON THE FACE

MIDDLE OF FOREHEAD *Prosperous; bad temper/cruel* ✳ LEFT TEMPLE *Spendthrift, headstrong* ✳ RIGHT TEMPLE *Capable* ✳ EYEBROW *Persevering, happy* ✳ RIGHT EYEBROW *Active & successful* ✳ OUTER CORNER EYE *Honest, reliable, needy* ✳ EAR *Wealth & fame, reckless* ✳ LEFT CHEEK *Serious, studious, struggling* ✳ RIGHT CHEEK *Successful* ✳ TIP OF NOSE *Sincere friend, hardworking* ✳ BRIDGE OF NOSE *Lust, extravagance* ✳ LEFT OF NOSE *Changeable, untrustworthy* ✳ RIGHT OF NOSE *Traveller, active* ✳ NOSTRILS *Wanderer* ✳ LIPS *Ambitious, greedy* ✳ LOWER LIP *Quiet, studious, fortunate later* ✳ CHIN *Conscientious, practical, adaptable, affectionate* ✳ LEFT LOWER JAW *Critical* ✳ RIGHT LOWER JAW *Danger from fire or water*

MOLES ON THE BODY

THROAT *Artistic, successful* ✳ FRONT OF NECK *Unexpected good fortune* ✳ SIDE OF NECK *Temperamental* ✳ BACK OF NECK *Desires a simple life* ✳ SHOULDER *Sensible, industrious* ✳ LEFT SHOULDER *Easy going* ✳ RIGHT SHOULDER *Prudent, discreet* ✳ SHOULDER BLADES *Restrictions* ✳ LEFT ARMPIT *Fortune from work* ✳ RIGHT ARMPIT *Struggles against odds* ✳ RIGHT ARM *Difficult early life, happy old age* ✳ LEFT ARM *Courteous, industrious* ✳ ELBOW *Talented, struggler, adventurer* ✳ HAND *Talented, successful* ✳ WRIST *frugal* ✳ RIGHT WRIST *Frugal, ingenious, dependable, successful* ✳ LEFT WRIST *Ingenious, artistic* ✳ FINGER *Dishonest, exaggerator, unrealistic* ✳ CHEST *Lazy, quarrelsome* ✳ RIGHT BREAST *Lazy, intemperate* ✳ LEFT BREAST *Active, energetic, fortunate* ✳ NIPPLE *Fickle, unfaithful* RIGHT RIBS *Insensitive, cowardly* ✳ LEFT RIBS *Lazy, humorous* ✳ NAVEL *Great fortune* ✳ ABDOMEN *Voracious, intemperate* ✳ BACK *Unreliable, untrustworthy* ✳ BUTTOCKS *Lack of ambition, complacent* ✳ GENITALS *Sex addict* ✳ HIP *Resourceful, valiant, amorous* ✳ LOINS *Dishonest* ✳ RIGHT THIGH *Wealth, happy marriage* ✳ LEFT THIGH *Warm natured* ✳ RIGHT KNEE *Friendly* ✳ LEFT KNEE *Rash, extravagant, ill tempered* ✳ RIGHT LEG *Energetic, persevering* ✳ LEFT LEG *Lazy* ✳ ANKLE *Kind, humorous* ✳ HEEL *Active, easily makes enemies & loses friends* ✳ RIGHT FOOT *Traveller* ✳ LEFT FOOT *Introspective, gloomy, sedentary* ✳ INSTEP *Athletic, quarrelsome*

ABOVE: A 1898 palmistry chart by Sivartha Alesha. Palmistry, or **CHIROMANCY**, reads lines in the palm of a person's hand as telling their life story. It is a practice found all over the world. Alexander the Great [356-323BC] famously studied the palms of his officers to gain insight into their characters.

RIGHT: Moleoscopy interprets the locations of moles for insights into luck and character.

ASTROLOGY
shining a light

ASTROLOGY is the study of how the sun, moon and planets influence life on earth. The Sun, the Moon and planets move along a path in the sky called the *ecliptic*, beyond which lie the twelve constellations of the *zodiac*. Early astronomers predicted planetary movements via complex tables and astrolabes, while astrologers interpreted their meaning.

There are many styles and applications of astrology, including: the election of auspicious timing for weddings, inaugurations, battles, operations, etc.; political analysis; cartography and the fortunes of location; prediction; horary divination of a chart constructed for a question; and natal astrology involving the analysis of a person's birth chart or horoscope to interpret their character and destiny.

A horoscope, from the Greek *hora* (time) and *skopos* (observer) is a map of the positions of the sun, moon and planets as observed from a particular place on earth at a particular time. The planets, originally thought of as gods and goddesses, each radiate specific types of energy, the signs of the zodiac representing different modes of expressing those energies and the houses (segments of sky) representing the spheres of life where these energies play out. Astrologers synthesise the unique pattern of the heavens at the birth of a person, enterprise or event to interpret their character, destiny and fortune (*see opposite and below*).

THE TWELVE HOUSES

1ST: *The body, the identity*	7TH: *Relationships and partner*
2ND: *Personal resources and self worth*	8TH: *Sex and death*
3RD: *Environment, neighbours and siblings*	9TH: *Travel and higher education*
4TH: *Home and security*	10TH: *Career and status*
5TH: *Children and creative expression*	11TH: *Friends, hopes and wishes*
6TH: *Work, health and service*	12TH: *Self undoing, institutions*

THE ASPECTS

♂ 0°: CONJUNCTION
∠ 45°: SEMISQUARE, *buggy*
✳ 60°: SEXTILE, *positive*
⬠ 72°: QUINT, *grow*

90°: SQUARE, *stressful* □
120°: TRINE, *harmony* △
135°: SESQUI, *careful* ⬚
144°: BIQUINT, *fizz* ✦
180°: OPPOSITION ☍

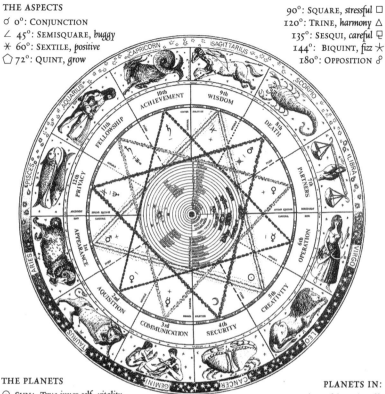

THE PLANETS

☉ SUN: *True inner self, vitality*
☽ MOON: *Responsive self, emotions*
☿ MERCURY: *Communication*
♀ VENUS: *Relationships and pleasure*
♂ MARS: *Aggression and energy*
♃ JUPITER: *Growth, benevolence and grace*
♄ SATURN: *Restriction, duty and learning*
♅ URANUS: *Freedom and breakthroughs*
♆ NEPTUNE: *Dissolution and mysticism*
♇ PLUTO: *Destruction and regeneration*
☊ NORTH MOON'S NODE: *Life's purpose*
☋ SOUTH MOON'S NODE: *Life's gifts*

PLANETS IN:

ARIES are assertive and impatient ♈
TAURUS are retentive, patient and acquisitive ♉
GEMINI are intellectual, quick and superficial ♊
CANCER are sensitive, clingy and protective ♋
LEO are bold, warm, creative and showy ♌
VIRGO are shy, self-analytic and helpful ♍
LIBRA are charming, balanced and fair ♎
SCORPIO are secretive and intense ♏
SAGITTARIUS are active and expansive ♐
CAPRICORN are ambitious and conservative ♑
AQUARIUS are humanitarian and independent ♒
PISCES are selfless and sensitive ♓

33

SELENOMANCY
by the light of the moon

SELENOMANCY is divination by the appearance and phases of the moon. Ancient markings on bones and cave walls show that lunar cycles were being recorded as far back as 25,000 BC. Timing activities according to the moon invites supportive energy for that endeavour, indeed gardening using the moon cycles is still widely practiced.

The moon passes through each of the twelve signs of the zodiac every lunar month as it orbits the earth. The phase of the moon (*below*), the position of the moon in the zodiac (*opposite*) plus important planetary transits and aspects all inform detailed forecasts of auspicious timings for contracts, weddings, purchases and periods of inactivity.

New Moon	First Quarter Moon	Full Moon	Final Quarter Moon	New Moon

1ST QUARTER　　2ND QUARTER　　3RD QUARTER　　4TH QUARTER

●●◐◑◐◑◐◑◐◑◐○○○○○○◑◐◑◐◑◐◑◐◑●●

NEW 338°-22°	CRESCENT 23°-67°	1st Q 68°-112°	WAX. GIBBOUS 113°-157°	FULL 158°-202°	WAN. GIBBOUS 203°-247°	4th Q 248°-292°	BALSAMIC 293°-337°
beginnings	*inspiration*	*action crisis*	*enthusiasm*	*power*	*reassessment*	*conscience*	*justice*
instinct	*clarity*	*balance*	*growth*	*completion*	*wisdom*	*contemplation*	*enemies*
health	*romance*	*motivation*	*building*	*magic*	*destruction*	*endings*	*obstacles*
improve	*planning*	*courage*	*dancing*	*change*	*protection*	*ancestors*	*removal*
creative	*firming up*	*friendship*	*acquisition*	*love*	*stress*	*prayer*	*separation*
lettuce	*cabbage*	*peas*	*tomatoes*	*onions*	*potatoes*	*weeding*	*digging*
endive	*spinach*	*beans*	*peppers*	*squash*	*berries*	*pests*	*rest*

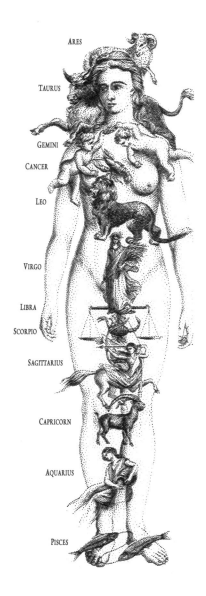

ARES

TAURUS

GEMINI

CANCER

LEO

VIRGO

LIBRA

SCORPIO

SAGITTARIUS

CAPRICORN

AQUARIUS

PISCES

LEFT; The signs of the zodiac assigned to different parts of the human body. The Moon rules Cancer, the crab, shown over the heart. For centuries, this concept was used to plan the timing of operations. For example, Aries is associated with the head, so Moon in Aries is not a good time to have brain surgery. Any day in which the Moon is void (makes no aspect to another body before leaving a zodiac sign) is also not ideal. Surgery is avoided when the Moon is in a mutable sign (Virgo, Gemini, Pisces or Sagittarius) and encouraged in fixed signs (Taurus, Leo, Scorpio or Aquarius). Operations are best five days before or after the new Moon, with fluids at their lowest ebb and less chance of swelling, and avoided five days before or after a full Moon when bodily fluids are at their highest with risk of swelling, haemorrhaging and wounds that won't heal.

NINE STAR KI
Japanese astrology

NINE STAR KI is a system of Japanese astrological cosmology, derived from the eight trigrams of the Chinese *Yi Jing* (*see page 18*). It is a system for determining one's natal element, using the Chinese five elements, and from that making predictions regarding travel, personality, health, relationship and environmental dynamics.

Chinese astronomers believed that Polaris, Vega and the seven stars of the Ursa Major system—the nine stars of Nine Star Ki—cause a slight 9-year fluctuation in the Earth's electromagnetic field. As the energy flow changes from year to year, one of the five elements becomes accentuated, giving rise to fire, earth, metal, water and wood years repeating in a 9-year cycle. This cycle is similarly reflected in smaller and larger increments, with cycles of nine, in months, days and hours.

水	土	木	木	土	金	金	土	火
I-WATER	2-EARTH	3-WOOD	4-WOOD	5-EARTH	6-METAL	7-METAL	8-EARTH	9-FIRE
1954	1953	1952	1951	1950	1949	1948	1947	1946
1963	1962	1961	1960	1959	1958	1957	1956	1955
1972	1971	1970	1969	1968	1967	1966	1965	1964
1981	1980	1979	1978	1977	1976	1975	1974	1973
1990	1989	1988	1987	1986	1985	1984	1983	1982
1999	1998	1997	1996	1995	1994	1993	1992	1991
2008	2007	2006	2005	2004	2003	2002	2001	2000
2017	2016	2015	2014	2013	2012	2011	2010	2009
2026	2025	2024	2023	2022	2021	2020	2019	2018
2035	2034	2033	2032	2031	2030	2029	2028	2027
2044	2043	2042	2041	2040	2039	2038	2037	2036

9 - FIRE - EXPANSION
PASSIONATE. clarity, charismatic, radiant, active, outgoing, clear opinions, sharp minds, can be lonely, vision, determined, impulsive, can be inconsiderate, impatient, thoughtless, self-confident.

8 - EARTH - MOUNTAIN
STRONG. Self reliant, can become isolated or stubborn, optimistic, spiritual quality, grace, stillness, proud, haughty, tenacious, may seem obstinate, gentle hearts, like adventure, tend to be possessive.

7 - METAL - LAKE
JOYFUL. Aware of aesthetics, sensitivity to life, easy talking, entertainers, social personalities, nervous, sometimes insincere, open and frank, practical, changeable, optimistic, may be bossy, good with money.

6 - METAL - HEAVEN
CREATIVE. Resilient, thinkers, efficient and highly organised minds, self-control, honest, direct, leadership, may be arrogant and dictatorial, not social, noble attitudes, not good at compromise, can offend.

5 - EARTH - PRIMAL POWER
GREAT CONTROLLER. Creative / destructive balance. At the centre of things, leaders, social, well respected, may be egotistical, confidence, vitality, bold, can have difficult early family life, tenacious.

4 - WOOD - WIND
MOVEMENT. Changeable. Independent, determined, generalists, desire for freedom & justice, indecisive, not practical, gentle, turbulent emotions, strength, impulsive, inspire confidence, giving nature.

3 - WOOD - THUNDER
EXPLOSIVE. Vibrant, sometimes threatening, poetic, idealistic, impulsive, bold, quick minds, easily frustrated, action oriented, can be rash, sensitive, determination, open and honest, self orientated, many projects.

2 - EARTH - EARTH
RECEPTIVE. Nurturers, quiet person of action, diligent, constant, hard working, conservative, relationships important, secure, thoughtful, can be perfectionists, supportive, service, like acknowledgment.

1 - WATER - WATER
DANGER. Gentle surface, strong inside, secretive, sensitive, deep thinkers, dreamers, easy going, good listeners, diplomatic, independent, adaptable, communicator, can be indecisive and lacking in clear direction.

ABOVE: Interpretations for each of the nine stars in Japanese Nine Star Ki.

LEFT: The Chinese Five Element system. In Nine Star Ki these elements are further expressed as being either Yin (black), Yang (white) or neutral (grey).

FACING PAGE: Look up your year number. The Chinese solar year starts on February 4 or 5, so if you were born before that date you need to subtract one from your year of birth.

WATER
feeling the vibes

WATER, THE ELEMENT OF THE SUBCONSCIOUS, is flowing, emotional, yielding, deep and penetrating. Foresight comes from tuning into the "etheric planes" and reading the energy signatures from objects, people, places, situations or sensory clues. This may come as snippets of knowing—sensed via the awakened third "eye of consciousness".

Divination through the water portal involves merging with the feeling of things rather than mental constructs. Unlike air and earth, the skill here is relaxing, letting go and using senses that may be beyond the rational. Development of this art is a very useful divinatory skill.

Even those professing no skills in the psychic arts can sense vibrations, feel the emotional undercurrent in a situation or place and perhaps see ghosts or auras. Being able to read the vibes of a being, object, place or situation will alert you to its health, wellbeing and suitability.

This can be applied even in mundane settings, such as choosing a seat at a restaurant, buying an antique, trusting a salesperson or assessing the health of a pet.

Water element divination includes DOWSING (*opposite*), ANTHOMANCY (*p.42*), PSYCHOMETRY (*p.40*), and SCRYING (*p.44*).

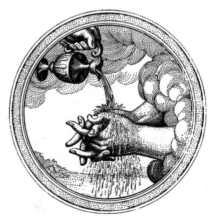

ABOVE: *A dowser looking for water or minerals using a traditional forked hazel branch. Dowsing uses subconscious senses to discover water, pipes, cables, lost pets, misplaced keys, food additives, the sex of an unborn babe, medical issues, earth energy lines and more.*

All sorts of things can serve as dowsing tools: L-rods (above) made from copper or an adapted wire coat hanger, a forked hazel branch (top), high-tech carbon fibre bobbers or a pendulum (right). L-rods have the advantage of working well for directional questions, such as "find me a clean earth energy spot in the back garden to place my bench." Your rods will show you the direction and then cross when you reach the spot.

To begin dowsing you need to establish a base line for responses. Put your device in a 'neutral position'. For a pendulum that is swinging gently back and forward. Ask to be shown a "yes" response (often a clockwise swing). Do the same for 'no'. Repeat the procedure a few times. Different dowsers have their own responses. Once you have established a system, your responses will stay the same for all similar devices.

PSYCHOMETRY
reading imprints

The vibrations or imprinted energy emanating from an object can at times be almost tangible. A focused reading such as **PSYCHOMETRY** can reveal information about previous owners or the use of an object. A seer may be able to pick up on the personality of the person linked with the item, their emotions and other factors—past, present and future.

A reader may receive information as a vision, emotion or subtle change of point of view. Any object can hold vibrations, but something personal that has been in close contact with the person, such as jewellery, is the most effective for reading. The energy of a building or space can also reveal information about former occupants and their activities.

With the object in front of you, put yourself in a meditative state, clearing yourself of any emotions and idle thoughts. Imagine yourself flooded with light before engaging with the object. Pick up the object and pay attention to your impressions, asking questions if needed.

Practice by tuning into an old piece of jewellery or clothing that you haven't worn for a while. See if it evokes memories and feelings. Or tune into an old door knocker in a junk shop to read if it belonged to a happy home. Modify your technique for distant readings. Use a photo of a place or person, touch a front door, or simply immerse yourself in the vibration of a space.

ANTHROMANCY
flower reading

ANTHROMANCY, or flower psychometry, appears widely in folklore. It is common knowledge, for example, that roses are the flower of love and beauty, that rosemary is for remembrance and lilies are for death.

One only reads flowers for another. The seeker must be drawn to the flower they choose, pick it freshly, hold it and tune into it for a minute or two. The seer, then receiving the flower, should steady themselves and link with the vibration of the flower. Describe what you feel as you move your fingers along the stem and onto the flower.

Leaves and flowers branching off of the main stem indicate diverging or competing interests and distractions, drives, hobbies, friends, family or work. Smooth stems suggest happiness, balance and understanding. A knot or bump on the stem warns of trouble, and isolation. Bigger lumps and breaks point to unresolved issues, relationships or addiction. Weak stems suggest sensitivity, fragility, anxiety and depression.

Notice how many flowers there are and examine their condition. Flower buds indicate patience and that which is yet to come, new opportunities in mundane matters such as money and work. A single large bloom represents an expansive nature, restless but open hearted and kind. Symmetrical flowers are chosen by people who like a sense of order, profuse blooms by those who love comfort and luxury, small flowers by homebodies and tiny single flowers by spiritual types.

CHART OF FLOWER MEANINGS

ACACIA: *Stability*
APRICOT: *Fruitfulness*
AGAPANTHUS: *Love*
ANEMONE: *Death*
ASPIDISTRA: *Fortitude*
AZALEA: *Passion*
BAMBOO: *Youth*
BLUEBELL: *Humility*
BUDDLEIA: *Profusion*
CARNATION: *Love*
CHAENOMELES: *Resolution*
CHERRY: *Fruitfulness*
CHINA ASTERS: *Fire*
CAMELLIA: *Evergreen*
CHRYSANTHEMUM: *Resolution*

CORNFLOWER: *Relationships*
CYCLAMEN: *Resignation*
CYPRESS: *Nobility*
DAFFODIL: *Hope & Contentment*
DAISY: *Loyalty & Innocence*
DELPHINIUM: *Consolidation*
EUONYMUS: *Modesty*
FORGET-ME-NOT: *Remembrance*
FORSYTHIA: *Vigour*
GARDENIA: *Loveliness*
GERANIUM: *Peacefulness*
GLADIOLI: *Severed ties*
HIBISCUS: *Profusion*
HOLLYHOCK: *Fertility*
HYDRANGEA: *Achievement*

HYPERICUM: *Profusion*
INCARVILLEA: *Flamboyance*
IVY: *Friendship*
JADE: *Wealth*
JASMINE: *Friendship*
JONQUIL: *Desire*
JUNIPER: *Tolerance*
KERRIA: *Individualism*
LILAC: *Virility*
LILIES: *Death*
MAGNOLIA: *Fragrance*
NANDINA: *Holiness*
NARCISSUS: *Rejuvenation*
NOMOCHARIS: *Tranquillity*
OLEANDER: *Everlasting love*
ORANGE: *Wealth*
ORCHID: *Endurance*
OSMANTHUS: *Evergreen*
PEACH: *Friendship*
PEAR: *Longevity*
PELARGONIUM: *Determination*
PEONY: *Wealth*
PETUNIA: *Anger*
PINE: *Longevity*
PLUM: *Youthfulness*
POMEGRANATE: *Fertility*
POPPY: *Eternal sleep*
PRIMROSE: *Youth*
PRIMULA: *Fire*
PYRACANTHA: *Vigour*
RHODODENDRON: *Delicacy*
RODGERSIA: *Profusion*
ROSE: *Beauty*
SAXIFRAGA: *Heavenly*

SORBUS: *Achievement*
SPIRAEA: *Marriage*
SUNFLOWER: *Follower*
SWEETPEA: *Pleasure & departure*
SYRINGA: *Fragrance*
THUJA: *Longevity*
TIGER LILY: *Wealth*
TULIP: *Love & devotion*
VIOLET: *Mourning*
VIRGINIA CREEPER: *Tenacity*
WATER LILY: *Fortitude*
WEIGELA: *Profusion*
WILLOW: *Grace*
WISTERIA: *Beauty*

SCRYING
mirror mirror

To **SCRY IS TO CONNECT** with the divine by gazing into a reflective surface. The earliest forms involved water; the Egyptians gazed into a pool of ink; the Babylonians gazed into various liquids in sacred bowls; the Hindus used bowls of molasses; ancient Greeks lowered mirrors into sacred wells and springs; the Chinese used polished bronze mirrors; Witches used blackened mirrors or polished onyx; Nostradamus used a brass bowl of water resting on a tripod and a looking glass.

Today the most popular form of scrying is **CRYSTALLOMANCY**, scrying with crystal balls. Some people use a lamen, an ornate circular table standing inside a magic circle, both inscribed with mystical names.

Use a sphere of about 4 inches (100mm) diameter made of beryl or quartz. Keep it wrapped, away from sunlight (moonlight is okay) and extremes of hot and cold. Ensure it is not handled by others.

Use a north-facing room with just enough light to read by. Place the crystal on the table or hold it in your hand, with a black cloth behind. Remove all distractions and gaze into the crystal. It should slowly fill with a milky hue, then go black before images are gradually revealed.

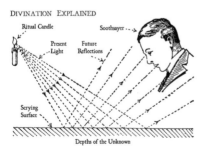

DIVINATION EXPLAINED

Ritual Candle — Soothsayer

Present Light — Future Reflections

Scrying Surface

Depths of the Unknown

INTERPRETING SYMBOLS

ANCHOR: *Safety, hope*
BEETLE: *Long life*
BIRD: *A message*
CROWN: *Glory, responsibility*
EYE: *Good fortune, also symbol of evil*
FRIEND: *Fertility, beneficial but hidden*
FRUIT: *Children, success*
GLOBE: *Travel, correspondance*
HEART PIERCED BY DAGGER: *Suffering*
LIGHTHOUSE: *Danger ahead, but hope*
MASK: *Deceit, tragedy*
SCALES: *Justice, even-handedness, or not*
SKULL: *Death, wisdom*
SNAKE: *Health, knowledge, temptation*
STAR: *Success, but be careful*
SWORDS: *A quarrel*
WATER LILLY: *Creativity*

INTERPRETING CLOUDS

WHITE: *Good fortune*
BLACK: *Ill fortune*
VIOLET, GREEN OR BLUE: *Joy*
RED, ORANGE OR YELLOW: *Danger*
ASCENDING CLOUDS: *Yes to your question*
DESCENDING CLOUDS: *No to your question*
CLOUDS MOVING TO RIGHT: *Spirits present*
CLOUDS MOVING LEFT: *Spirits have departed*

INTERPRETING EVENTS

AT FRONT OF CRYSTAL: *Relates to the present or immediate future*
AT BACK OF CRYSTAL: *Relates to the remote past or distant future*
TO YOUR LEFT: *Events are real*
TO YOUR RIGHT: *Events are symbolic*

ABOVE: *Interpreting your scrying results.*
LEFT: *1920s poster.* FACING PAGE: LEFT: *Divination explained, after Craig Conley.*
RIGHT: *Scrying, Lustige Blätter, 1902.*

ETHER
Heaven's gift

ETHER IS THE FORCE that ties together the other elements and all that is. It is beyond action, manifestation, thinking and feeling. The insights that arrive via ether may be unbidden and even unwelcome, such as dreams, premonitions and precognition. Some people are gifted with the ability to consciously draw from other planes of awareness, but this is a skill that can also be developed through focus, practice and training.

Connecting with the ethers is a pursuit shared by many different cultures and within shamanic practices, where seers achieve heightened states in rituals involving trancing, ecstatic dance, drumming and the use of entheogenic herbs, such as ayahuasca and mushrooms.

Divination using the ethers includes PSYCHISM (CLAIRVOYANCE, CLAIRAUDIENCE and CLAIRSENTIENCE, *opposite*), ASTRAL PALACE (*p.49*), AURA READING (*p.50*), CHANNELLING (*p.52*), DREAM WALKING (*p.48*) and VISION QUESTS (*p.54*).

LEFT: *Siberian Shaman with drum.*
BELOW: *PSYCHISM, or second sight, includes CLAIRVOYANCE, the power to see what is hidden, CLAIRAUDIENCE, hearing what is normally inaudible, and CLAIRSENTIENCE, a kind of super-feeling super-empathy.*

We live surrounded by a vast sea of ether to which we are mostly insensitive. Second sight is the ability to extend consciousness beyond the five senses into the vibrations of the other planes.

Etheric perception intensifes colours, feelings and hearing. Walls can become transparent. You may glimpse coloured clouds, pathways to other landscapes and dimensions and even the magnetic field of etheric energy that surrounds humans, animals, trees and rocks.

You may meet nature spirits and elementals: fairies, plant spirits and gnomes; as well as other energetic constructs and thought forms from the astral realms who can pop in and out at specific times and locations in the more visible form of etheric matter: ghosts, entities, ghouls and other denizens of the lower astral, either haunting places or people, or just passing through after a death.

Oneiromancy
a dream within a dream

Dream divination has been a source of prophecy widely practised by all cultures. In dreams we walk the astral and causal planes and can tap into what Carl Jung [1875–1961] called the collective unconscious.

PSYCHIC DREAMING takes many forms: VISITATION DREAMS where a message is received, EMPATHY DREAMS which precipitate change, PRECOGNITIVE and WARNING DREAMS and TEACHING DREAMS.

Some people know they are dreaming. LUCID DREAMING allows a dreamer to direct their dream and consult with mages, guides, etc. Practice REALITY TESTING (*see caption opposite*) to dream more lucidly.

DREAM WALKING incubates dreams targeted to a specific question. Before dropping off to sleep, mentally run through the day's events in reverse order. Then ask your question and go to sleep with it on your mind. Remember to keep writing equipment by your bed.

SHE·SLEEPS·A·CHARMED·SLEEP

LEFT: *Drawing by Florence Harrison, 1910.*
BELOW: *Woodcut by Gwen Raverat, 1910.*
OPPOSITE: *Drawing by Miriam English, 1977.*

One pathway to the astral planes is to imagine an ASTRAL PALACE *or garden. Begin with a guided meditation (see p.54), then give it more structure and life. Persistent creative thoughts will form a corresponding astral body, so as you add more details, your Palace will become more and more substantial. You can visit it at will and use it as a source of wisdom, knowledge and prophesy, inviting guides to work with you there. Use it as a gateway to access other astral lands and experiences.*

FACING PAGE: *Awake into a lucid dream using* REALITY TESTING. *While awake, click your fingers and read some text while trying to pass your hand through a table or door. When dreaming it's easy to pass your hand through a door but hard to click and read text. Practice often while you are awake to remind yourself to repeat it when asleep, when it will act as a trigger to propel you into a lucid state. You can also pop a dream sachet of mugwort, lavender, hops, chamomile, lemon balm, rosemary, cloves or lemon verbena under your pillow to help. Set an alarm to wake you 5-6 hours after bedtime and then let yourself go back to sleep, straight into a cycle of REM dreaming.*

AURA READING
seeing double

We are, in essence, an unfolding dance of cosmic dust. The aura is an energy phenomenon in an interwoven and complex network, which sustains, protects and informs our physical self, while connecting us to the great cosmic loom. It offers an excellent window to our mental, physical and spiritual wellbeing.

Although the basic structure of the aura is relatively fixed (*see opposite*) it is highly sensitive to emotional, physiological, social and environmental factors, and contains a chronicle of one's entire life.

To read an aura, place your subject in front of an off-white wall in natural indirect lighting. Stand about 10ft (3m) away and focus on a point on their forehead. Now expand your awareness to your peripheral vision while still looking at the point.

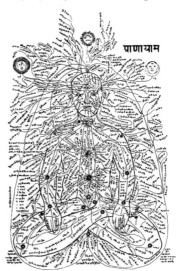

Allow your focus to become soft. A white energetic halo will pop into view around the subject. Look beyond this and the details of the aura will come into view.

Colour and vibrancy are two of the most noticeable qualities of the human aura, and each has a story to tell (*see opposite*). Psychic impressions and insights into health and emotional issues may also appear while reading the aura.

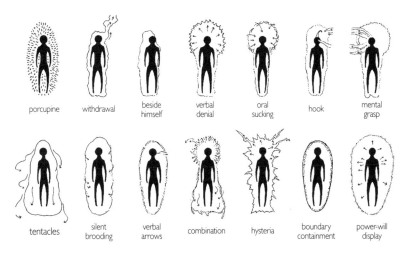

porcupine   withdrawal   beside himself   verbal denial   oral sucking   hook   mental grasp

tentacles   silent brooding   verbal arrows   combination   hysteria   boundary containment   power-will display

ABOVE: *The Aura as a varied defense system. A person's aura can tell you a lot about them.*
FACING PAGE: *The subtle body involves meridian lines and chakra centres which power the aura.*

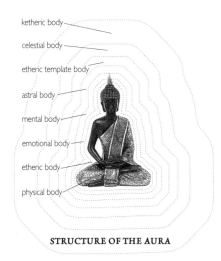

ketheric body
celestial body
etheric template body
astral body
mental body
emotional body
etheric body
physical body

STRUCTURE OF THE AURA

COLOURS IN THE AURA

YELLOW: *intelligent, dependable, sociable*
LIGHT BLUE: *balance, insightful, optimism*
DEEP BLUE: *sharp intellect, self-discipline*
BRIGHT GREEN: *healing, caring, enlightened*
DULL GREEN: *inner turmoil, pessimism, envy*
IRIDESCENT GREEN: *psychic, magic workers*
PINK: *youth, idealism, longevity*
BROWN: *practical, independent (also smoke)*
PURPLE: *creative, philosophical, intelligent*
ORANGE: *achievers, extroverts, competitive*
DULL ORANGE: *impatient, egotistic, unstable*
RED: *anger, aggression, violence*
GREY: *Forewarns crisis, adversity or illness*

CHANNELLING
is there anybody out there?

Channelling is a technique for contacting spirits of the dead, guides and angelic beings. Channellers enter an altered state of awareness and open themselves to receive messages like a relay centre for otherworldly messages. Others, who work with spirit, such as shamans, pagans, psychics and mediums, may receive auditory, empathic or visual messages. Similar practices, including séances (*below*), mediumship (*lower, opposite*), automatic writing (*opposite, top right*) and drawing, are allied techniques for pulling in spirit messages. All such techniques have different traditions and rituals but essentially share the same process.

As the astral planes are populated by all types of beings, it is important to be aware of protection protocols (*see page 4*) before attempting to communicate with these realms. When spirit beings initiate contact with you it is wise to be wary, as they may have dubious agendas and a poor quality of information.

TOP LEFT: *Parlour games using the Ouija board became very popular in the late 19th and early 20th century. Think of a question, write it down and relax your body and mind allowing the writing to flow spontaneously.*

FACING PAGE: *Victorian holiday entertainments and parties would often include a séance to communicate with the dead – a form of* **NECROMANCY**.

TOP RIGHT: *Automatic writing allows a seer to produce words without consciouslessly writing. It has a long tradition In China, where it is known as Fuji, or spirit writing.*

LEFT: *Alphonse Mucha, from Le Pater (1889). Some seers work in a mild trance state while others need an elaborate ritual to enter a deeper trance. Following a request for contact with a spirit being, contact may feel like an sense of love, the presence of a wise being or a vision of serendipity.*

VISION QUEST
into the mystic realms

A **VISION QUEST** is a rite of passage, a journey of self-discovery into the spirit realms for healing, connecting with life purpose and stepping into one's own power. The aim is to seek divine revelation and connect with your higher self, guides, totems and allies. Traditionally, a quest might include cleansing rituals, fasting, energy raising activities, meditation practices and the use of entheogenic herbs, undertaken in a group with experienced guides in a natural setting.

There are many ways to make the journey. You may find a teacher, participate in a working group, climb a mountain or simply dedicate time to contemplate in the stillness of a natural environment or a sacred space. The way you frame your journey will colour your experience. The form of the ritual facilitates the "heroic step" through the open door and onto the spirit path that connects you to your own mystical dimensions. Undertake your own quest using these guidelines:

Clear your mind ◊ Visualise a symbol for your quest emblazoned on a double door in front of you ◊ See the doors open and see the realm beyond ◊ Walk through the doors and follow the spirit path before you ◊ Observe every detail of your journey, noting all landscapes and beings you encounter ◊ Accept any gifts or wisdoms offered with gratitude ◊ When you are to return, go back the way you came, through the doors and back into your physical body.

APPENDIX - TYPES OF DIVINATION

A - **ABACOMANCY**: Divn. by dust. **ACULTOMANCY**: Divn. by needles. **AEROMANCY**: Divn. by atmospheric conditions such as clouds, wind, thunder, lightning and other meteorological phenomena. **AGALMATOMANCY**: Divn. from statues. **AICHMOMANCY**: Divn. from sharp objects. **AILUROMANCY**: Divn. from cats. **ALECTRYOMANCY**: Augury involving the eating patterns of sacred chickens. **ALEUROMANCY**: Divn. using flour. **ALOMANCY**: Divn. using salt. **ALPHITOMANCY**: Special cakes made of barley flour. **ALVEROMANCY**: Divn. by sound. **AMATHOMANCY**: Divn. using sand: **AMBULO-MANCY**: Divn. by walking. **AMNIOMANCY**: Divn. from placenta. **ANEMOSCOPY**: Divn. from the wind. **ANTHO-MANCY**: Divn. from flowers: **ANTHRACOMANCY**: By reading burning coals. **ANTHROPOMANCY**: Divn. from a human sacrifice. **ANTHROPOSCOPY**: By reading physical attributes in humans. **APANTOMANCY**: Omens from things that present themselves by chance, especially animals, such as a black cat crossing your path. **ARACHNOMANCY**: The appearance and behaviour of spiders. **ARCHEOMANCY**: Reading sacred antiquities: **ARIOLATION**: Divn. from altars. **ARITHOMANCY**: Numerology of words and phrases. **ARUSPICINA**: By examining entrails. **ASPIDOMANCY**: Channelling while sitting on a shield or in a circle. **ASTRAGALOMANCY**: Divn. by casting the knuckle bones of sheep (see too reading with dice, cleromancy & astragyromancy). **ASTRAPOMANCY**: Reading lightning flashes. **ASTROLOGY**: Divn. using stars and planets, their patterns and cycles. **AUGURY**: Divn. from the appearance of bird formations. **AUROMANCY**: By reading auras. **AUSPICY**: By observing birds. Also avimancy. **AUSTROMANCY**: Divn. from the wind. **AXIOMANCY**: Divn. from axes: **B** - **BAZI**: Chinese Astrology also known as Four Pillars. **BELOMANCY**: Divn. by arrows. **BIBILOMANCY**: Divn. from books, including rhapsodomancy, also called stichomancy. **BLETONOMANCY**: By observing water currents. **BOTANOMANCY**: Pyromancy by burning leaves and branches. **BRIZOMANCY**: Dream Divn. **BRONTOMANCY**: Divn. from thunder. **BUMPOLOGY**: By reading bumps. **C** - **CANOMANCY**: Divn. from dogs. **CAPNOMANCY**: Pyromancy by smoke. **CARTOMANCY**: Divn. using modern playing cards related to tarot. **CATOPTROMANCY**: Scrying using a mirror. **CAUSINOMANCY**: Pyromancy by objects cast into the fire. **CEPHALOMANCY**: Augury from the skull or head of a donkey or goat. **CERAUNOSCOPY**: Aeromancy using thunder and lightning. **CEROMANCY**: Divn. from melted wax. **CHALOMANCY**: Divn. by the sounding of gongs and bowls. **CHAOMANCY**: Aeromancy using aerial visions. **CHINESE ASTROLOGY**: Divn. based on a 12-year cycle and involving the 12 animals of Shengxiao, which, unlike the zodiac signs of Western astrology, are not based on the configuration or movement of planets or stars. **CHIROMANCY**: Divn. using the palm of the hand including an analysis of hand shape, fingers, and fingernails; also called chirgnomy, chirology, or palmistry. **CHORIOMANCY**: By reading pig's bladders. **CHRESMOMANCY**: Divn. by the ravings of a lunatic. **CLAIRAUDIENCE**: A form of clairvoyance by hearing. **CLAIRVOYANCE**: Divn. by seeing the future ahead of time. Different forms are clairaudience, metagnomy, precognition. **CLAMANCY**: A reading from the random shouts of a crowd. **CLEDONOMANCY**: Divn. by chance happenings or rumours. **CLEIDOMANCY**: A form of radiesthesia or dowsing using a suspended key. **CLEROMANCY**: By casting lots, also Divn. with dice Also astrgalomancy. **COMETOMANCY**: Divn. from the tails of comets. **CONCHOMANCY**: A reading from shells. **COSCINOMANCY**: Dowsing using a suspended device. **COSQUINOMANCY**: Divination from hanging sieves. **COTTABOMANCY**: Divination by wine in a bowl. **CRITHOMANCY**: Reading the markings on freshly baked bread. **CROMNIOMANCY**: A reading from onion sprouts: **CRYPTOMANCY**: Divining omens from hidden messages.

CRYOMANCY: A reading from ice. CRYSTALLOMANCY: Scrying with a crystal ball. CYATHOMANCY: Divn. using cups. CYBERMANCY: Divn. using computer technology. CYCLICOMANCY: Divn. from swirling water in a cup. CYCLOMANCY: A reading using wheels. **D** - DACTYLIOMANCY: Dowsing with a suspended ring. DACTYLOMANCY: Reading finger movements. DAPHNOMANCY: A form of pyromancy, the burning of laurel leaves. DENDROMANCY: A reading from trees particularly oaks, yews or mistletoes. DOBUTSU URANAI: Modern Japanese Divn. based on date of birth assigning an animal type and personality. DOWSING: Divn. using a pendulum, L rods or traditionally a forked hazel twig; different forms include cleidomancy, coscinomancy, and dactylomancy; also called radiesthesia. DOMINOMANCY: Divn. using dominoes. DRIMIMANCY: Divn. using bodily fluids. **E** - ELEOMANCY: Divn. using oil. ENTOMOMANCY: Augury from the appearance and behaviour of insects. FAVOMANCY: Divn. from beans. FEI XING GONG FA: Divn. using the principles of Chinese metaphysics. GEOMANCY: Divn. by the patterns in the earth, also the practice of reading and enhancing the built and natural environment. **F** - FENG SHUI: Chinese art of reading and harmonising the environment. FLORAMANCY: A reading from a fresh flower or plant picked by the seeker. **G** - GELOSCOPY: A reading from laughter. GRAPHOLOGY: Assessment of a person's character from handwriting. **H** - HAKATA: African method of casting carved bones. HALOMANCY: Pyromancy by casting salt into a fire. HARUSPICY: Augury from the entrails and body part of animals. HEPATOSCOPY: Haruspicy using the liver. HIEROMANCY: Divn. from the entrails of a sacrifice. HIPPOMANCY: Divn. from horses. HORARY: Divn. from an astrological chart drawn at the moment of the question. HYDROMANCY: Scrying by water. HYOMANCY: Divn. from wild hogs. **I** - I CHING: Chinese method of Divn., Mandarin is Yi Jing, also known as the Book of Changes. ICHNOMANCY: Reading footprints. ICHTHYOMANCY: Augury from the shape and entrails of fish. IFA: An African method of geomancy. IRIDOLOGY: A reading from the iris of the eye. **J** - JIAOBEI: A Chinese Divn. tool. Wooden moon blocks tossed in pairs to give a yes/no answer. Also known as poe. JYOTISH: Vedic astrology, claimed to the oldest form of astrology. **K** - KAU CIM: Chinese fortune sticks where a box is shaken until one stick falls out to give a reading. Also Chien Tung or qiantong. KIPPER CARDS: A German card deck with very literal meanings rather than the symbolic and intuitive forms of tarot cards. KNISSOMANCY: Divn. from the vapours of incense. Also libanomancy. **L** - LAMPADOMANCY: Divn. using an oil lamp or a torch flame. LECANOMANCY: Divination from a basin of water. LENORMAND: A popular card deck in France and Germany invented in the 1850 named after the fortune teller Marie Anne Adelaide Lenormand. LITHOMANCY: Divn. using gem stones. LYCHNOMANCY: Divn. from the flames of candles. **M** - MACHAROMANCY: Divn. using knives. MARGARITOMANCY: Divn. from pearls. MAHJONG: A reading using mah-jong tiles. METAGNOMY: Hypnotic trance originally evolved for predicting malady and cure. METEORMANCY: Aeromancy using meteors and shooting stars. METOPOSCOPY: Divn. from lines on the forehead. MI KAYU URA: Japanese Shinto Divn. ritual using rice or bean gruel to predict the weather and harvests for the year. MOLEOSCOPY: Assessing character from moles on the body. Also meilomancy. MOLYBDOMANCY: Divn. using molten metals. MYOMANCY: Divn. from the colour and movement of mice. MYRMOMANCY: Interpreting the behaviour of ants. **N** - NECROMANCY: Communing with the dead using automatic writing, a ouija board, or through a psychic. NECYOMANCY: Summoning the dead; a type of necromancy associated with the dark arts. NEPHOMANCY: Divn. from clouds. NGGAM: Divn. from Cameroon and Nigeria using the actions of spiders and crabs. NUMEROLOGY: Numbers of letters and objects are analysed to understand lives and personality; also called numeromancy or arithomancy. NUMISMATOMANCY: Divn. using coins. **O** - OCULOMANCY: Divn. from the eyes. Also iridology. OENOMANCY:

Divn. from the patterns made by wine. **OGHAM**: Celtic inspired Divn. using "staves", wood from sacred trees carved with the Ogham alphabet. **OLOLYGMANCY**: Divn. from the howling of dogs. **OMIKUJI**: Japanese fortune paper strips, literally meaning "sacred lot", drawn at a temple. Similar to Chinese Kau cim: **ONEIROMANCY**: Divn. using dreams. **OOMANCY**: Divn. from eggs. **OPHIOMANCY**: Augury from the colour and movement of snakes. **ORNITHOMANCY**: Divn. using the sound, appearance and flight of birds. **OSTEOMANCY**: Bone reading. **OUIJA**: A spirit board with marks such as the alphabet used to communicate with the dead. **P** - **PALLOMANCY**: Dowsing with a pendulum. **PALMISTRY**: Divn. using the palm of the hand, which also includes an analysis of hand shape, fingers, and fingernails; also called chirognomy, chirology, or chiromancy. **PEGOMANCY**: Hydromancy using a sacred pool or spring. **PESSOMANCY**: Divn. by drawing or casting of specially marked pebbles; also called psephomancy. **PHYLLOMANCY**: Divn. from leaves. **PHYLLORHODOMANCY**: Divn. using rose petals. **PHRENOLOGY**: Assessing character from the presence of bumps on the head. **PHYSIOGNOMY**: Character analysis using physical features. **PLASTROMANCY**: A reading from the cracks formed by heating a turtle's plastron. **PODOMANCY**: Reading the soles of feet. **PRECOGNITION**: A form of clairvoyance giving knowledge of the future. **PSYCHOMETRY**: A form of clairvoyance where holding an object gives you information about the people and history connected to the object. **PSYCHOGRAPHY**: Channelling spirit using automatic writing. **PTARMOSCOPY**: Divn. by interpreting sneezes. **PYROMANCY**: Divn. by fire; different forms include, botanomancy, capnomancy, causinomancy, daphnomancy, halomancy, pyroscopy, and sideromancy. **PYROSCOPY**: Pyromancy by burning a sheet of paper on a white surface and examining the resulting stains. **R** - **RADIESTHESIA**: French for Dowsing. **RHABDOMANCY**: Divining or dowsing for water or minerals using rods or wands. **RHAPSODOMANCY**: A form of bibliomancy from poetry. **ROADOMANCY**: Reading star constellations. **RUNES**: The symbols of an ancient alphabet that are used for Divn. **S** - **SCAPULOMANCY**: Augury from the patterns or cracks and fissures on the burned shoulder blade of an animal. **SCRYING**: Divn. by gazing into a reflective surface. There are many different forms, including crystallomancy, catoptromancy, and hydromancy. **SEANCE**: A meeting of people typically led by a medium who communicate with the dead or astral spirits. **SELENOMANCY**: Divn. from the moon. **SHUFFLEMANCY**: Divn. using the shuffle function on a digital media player. **SIDEROMANCY**: Pyromancy by burning straws on red hot iron and reading the patterns, movements, flames and smoke. **SKATHAROMANCY**: Interpreting beetle tracks. **SORTES VERGILIANAE**: A form of bibliomancy from works of the Roman poet Virgil. **SORTILEGE**: Divination by the casting or drawing of lots; different types include astragalomancy, belomancy, bibliomancy, pessomancy (also known as psephomancy), rhapsodomancy, and stichomancy. It is also called cleromancy. **STERCOMANCY**: Divn. using the seeds in bird droppings. **STICHOMANCY**: Divn. using books. Also called bibliomancy. **STOICHEOMANCY**: From the Iliad and the Odyssey. **T** - **TAROMANCY**: A reading using tarot cards. **TASSEOGRAPHY**: Divn. from a cup using tea leaves or coffee grounds. **TELAESTHESIA**: Interpreting of physical disturbances of the body, such as throbbing, twitching, itching or whistling in the ears. **TEPHROMANCY**: Divn. from the ashes of ritual and sacrifice fires. **THEOMANCY**: The consulting of an oracle that is inspired by the gods, such as the Oracle of Delphi. **THERIOMANCY**: Divn. from the behaviour of animals. **TURIFUMY**: By interpreting the shapes in smoke. **TYROMANCY**: Divination from cheese. **U** - **UMBROMANCY**: Divn. using shade. **UROMANCY**: Divn. using urine. **URTICARIAOMANCY**: Divn. from itches (see telaesthesia). **W** - **WATER DIVINING**: Dowsing for underground water (also called water witching). **X** - **XYLOMANCY**: Divn. using wood, such as twigs, branches or logs. **Z** - **ZOOMANCY**: Augury from the appearance and behaviour of any animal.